QUICK DIVE
INTO
AZURE WEB APPS

What to Expect

The goal of this book is to provide a quick overview of Microsoft Azure Web Apps. Starting from cloud fundamentals to deep dive in web apps, this book provides an easy to follow, step by step guide to web apps in Azure. I strongly recommend readers of this book to practice along and get some hands-on experience.

Why you should buy this book:

a) For a quick overview of web apps in Microsoft Azure.
b) Free Support: You can email me at cloudsimplifiedforyou@gmail.com for any questions (technical or related to book) you may have. Typically, I will answer your question in 1-2 business days. Please limit your questions to topics discussed in this book. Thank you, kindly.

Table of Contents

Chapter One - Introduction to Cloud

The goal of this chapter is to get you started with cloud. First, we will understand basics of cloud computing and then we will do some real work in Azure Resource Manager.

Cloud computing has gained popularity over the last few years. A lot of companies have switched to cloud. In cloud computing data is stored and accessed over the internet. As you read this book you will understand how you can make your application scalable, reliable and reduce overall cost by moving it to cloud.

In a traditional architecture, all the servers are on premise. What that means is all the infrastructure is within four walls of company's datacenter. Company is responsible for maintaining it. They will purchase hardware, databases(s) and any additional infrastructure needed to run software's. Most of the companies will have a dedicated team to maintain these resources. If there is a need to increase number of production or test servers, this team will order new servers, wait for them to arrive and then they will install all pre-requisite software's on these servers. It can take anywhere from few weeks to months, before developers can get a chance to publish their website on these servers.

Though the traditional architecture gives more control on the resources, it is not easily scalable and costs more. Say you are working for a big retail company named "ABC". You have developed a website for their order management system. You have one Dev and two QA servers dedicated for your website. Everything is running smoothly. One day your manager asks you to learn and integrate a new software in your website and do some testing. He has allocated four weeks for you to complete this task. You are very excited about learning this new software and integrating it with your website. You go through the documentation, learn new software, make some changes to your website on your local machine and now you are ready to deploy these changes on server and show it to your manager. The problem is you cannot deploy in your current dev server as other developers are using it. So, you need a new server. However, buying a new server for such a small task may not be a wise option. Therefore, you are left scratching your head and with not many options on table you may end up ordering new servers. Let us see how this problem can be solved by migrating applications to cloud.

Cloud service providers like Microsoft and Amazon provide all the resources within their datacenters. Instead of paying cost upfront, you pay as you go. The service provider will be responsible for providing resources on demand, security, and core networking functions. They have datacenters all around the world. Going back to the scenario we discussed earlier, if your website is in cloud, you can increase the number of app servers for a specific period, pay for the time you use these servers and then take them out. Your total cost will be very less as compared to cost of buying new servers. Moreover, you do not have to worry about maintenance of servers.

Let us take another example to see how moving to cloud can help us. You developed a new website and deployed it in cloud. First month as you are still getting it all set up, traffic will be low. So, maybe you just need one instance (Server). As your website starts to gain popularity, you will eventually need more servers. Consider yourself fortunate that your website is in cloud. Cloud gives us the flexibility to configure number of instances we can have based on the demand. We can set up conditions that can automatically add or reduce the number of servers based upon traffic.

Depending on your requirement you can choose from the following types of service model provided by the service providers:

SaaS (Software as Service)

SaaS is defined as software that is deployed over the Internet. In SaaS, third party provider hosts applications. Users can connect to applications via internet. It is also referred to as on demand software.

Example: Outlook.

PaaS (Platform as a Service)

PaaS is a computing platform that enables quick and easy creation of web applications. With PaaS, you can easily deploy your web applications. Service provider will provide the resources on demand. You do not have to buy or maintain the infrastructure. You can create your own web application and deploy it over cloud. You can choose size of underlying virtual machines for your app. However, you do not have full control over these machines. For example, you cannot remote desktop into them or do operations like an administrator, though you can still access logs.

Example: Salesforce Heroku

IaaS (Infrastructure as a service)

IaaS allows organizations to have complete control over their infrastructure. They have direct access to servers and storage. However, instead of buying all the infrastructure upfront, organizations will buy resources as a service on demand. This gives them the flexibility and allow them to set up virtual machines, install software's, set up load balancers and network security groups.

Note: IaaS clients are responsible for managing everything from operating system to application.

Azure Subscription – if you are new to Azure, first step for you is to create an Azure account. You can get $200 credit to try any combination of Azure services. Isn't that great? Check out this link for more information: https://Azure.microsoft.com/en-us/free/

Azure Resources – Anything that we create in Azure such as Virtual Machine, App Service, is an Azure resource.

Resource Group – A resource group is a container into which Azure resources are deployed and can be managed. In other words, it is for grouping resources that work together. For example, if you have a website that connects to a database then this website and database can be put together in one resource group. If you delete this resource group, then both website and database will be deleted. Resource groups make maintenance of underlying resources easier. You do not have to delete resources one by one. Delete the resource group and it will take care of all resources that are in that resource group. You can also control access to all the resources under resource group. Another advantage of using resource group is that you can use templates (JSON File) to create all resources under your resource group.

Exercise 1: Create a new Resource Group

In this exercise, we will learn how to create a resource group. If you have not created your free Azure account yet, then I recommend you do it and practice along.

When you log in into your Microsoft Azure account, you will see "Resource groups" link in your dashboard. To create a new resource group, click on this link.

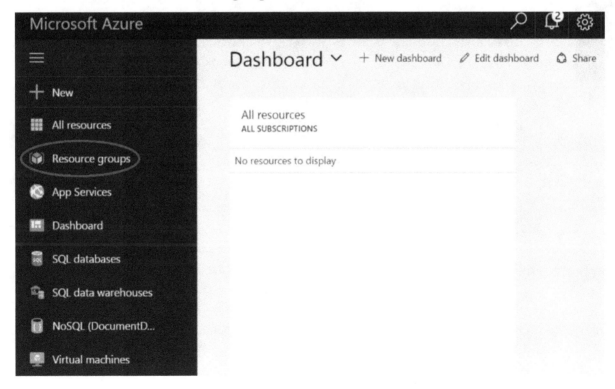

7

After you click "Resource groups" you will be presented with a display shown below. Microsoft calls these pages as blades. Please note that Microsoft is constantly making changes to these pages (blades), so it is possible that you may see some differences between the snapshot presented below and the blade you are viewing in Azure.

On this page, you can see all existing resource groups and you have an option to create a new one. Since, we have not created any resource groups yet so you will see the following message "No resource groups to display". For this exercise, we are going to create a new resource group. Click on the "+Add" link.

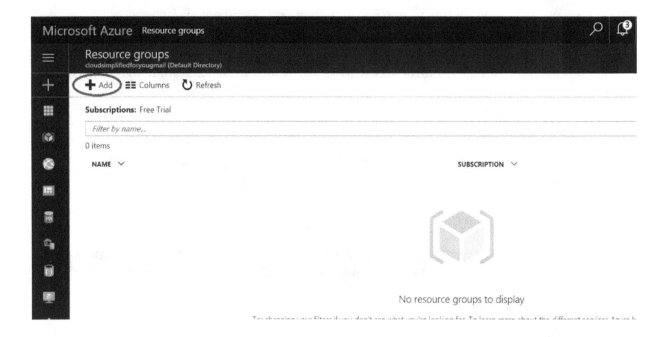

After you click "+Add", you will be taken to the following page.

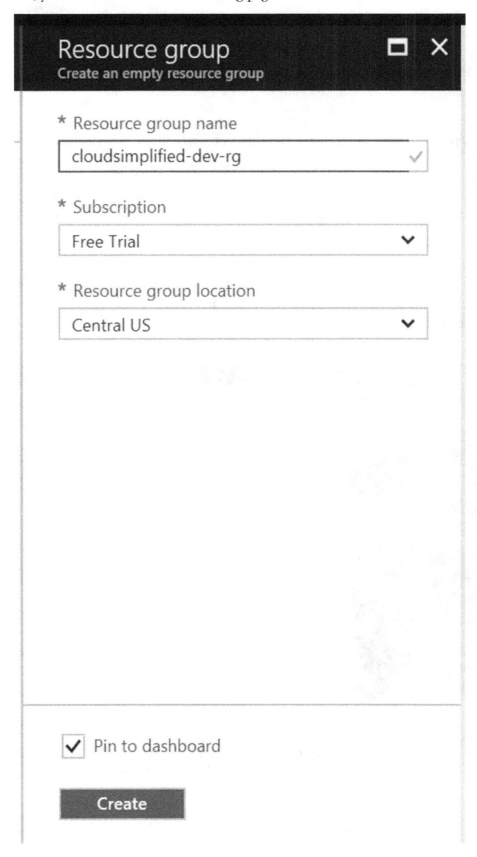

Enter resource group name, subscription and select resource group location. It is always a good practice to follow naming conventions while naming resources. As number of resources grow, it will be easy for you to recognize type of resource just by looking at the name. The resource group stores metadata about the resources. This metadata will be stored at the location you select when creating a resource group. For this exercise enter "cloudsimplified-dev-rg" as name and select "Central US" as location. Click on the "Create" button to create a resource group.

App Service Plan

An app service plan represents collection of physical resources to host apps. All apps that are in the same app service plan will share resources. This means if we have 5 apps assigned to the same app service plan and we have 2 virtual machines in the plan then all these 5 apps will be hosted on these two virtual machines. So, instead of hosting each app on a separate virtual machine, app service plan allows us to reduce overall cost by hosting multiple apps on same set of virtual machines.

Exercise 2: Create a new App Service Plan

In this exercise, we are going to create a new app service plan. If you are not able to see app service plans link in your dashboard, then you can search for it. Type App service plans in the search resources textbox. As you start typing "App service plans" in the textbox, azure portal will try to auto complete your search and show you possible options. As you see "App Service plans" option you can click on it. It will take you to app service plan page.

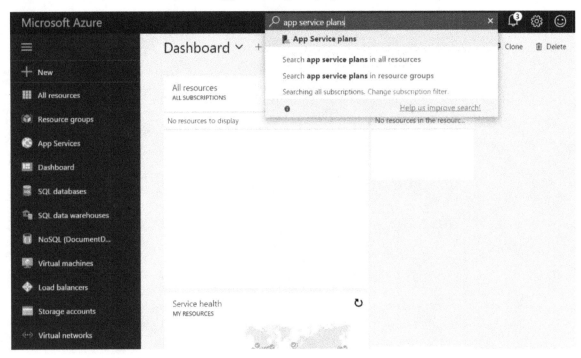

Once you are on app service plan page, you can see any existing app service plans associated to your subscription. As you can see below, I have a plan named "cloudsimplifiedserviceplan". It does not have any app associated to it. To create a new app service plan, click on the "+Add" link.

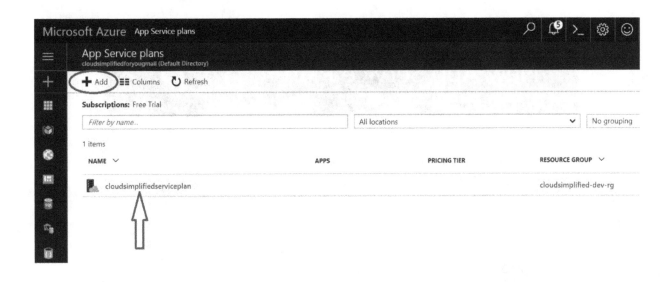

After you click "+Add" you will be presented with the following page.

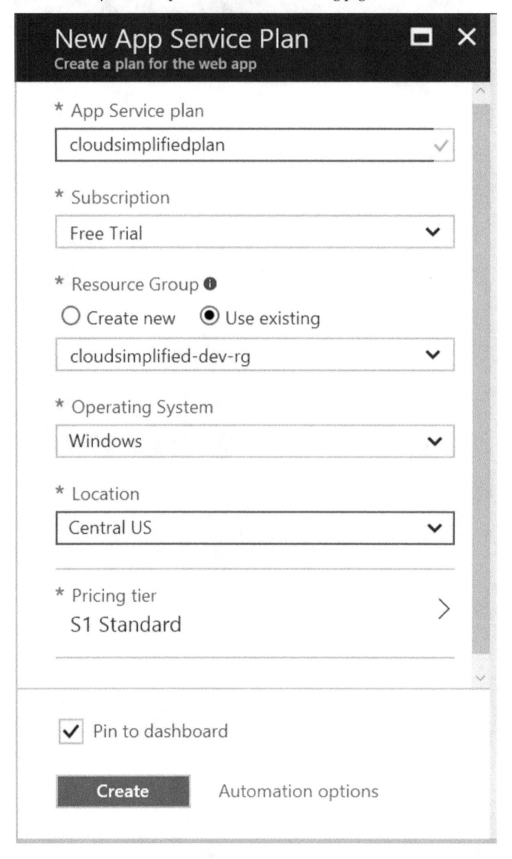

To create a new app service plan, you will enter app service plan, select subscription, create or use existing resource group, select location and pricing tier. We will talk about pricing tier later. As you can see there is a "Pin to dashboard" checkbox. If you check it and then click on the "Create" button, app service plan option will start appearing on your dashboard and you do not have to search for it. For this exercise, you can enter name as "cloudsimplifiedplan", select resource group as "cloudsimplified-dev-rg", location as "Central US" and select pricing tier as "S1 Standard". Click on the "Create" button to create app service plan.

Exercise 3: Delete an App Service Plan

In this exercise, I will show you how to delete an app service plan. We are going to delete app service plan named "cloudsimplifiedserviceplan".

Note: You can only delete an app service plan that is not associated to any web app. If a plan is associated to a web app then you must first delete web app and then delete app service plan.

Go to app service plans page, click on "…" text to open context menu. Then click on the "Delete" link to delete this app service plan.

Chapter Two: App Services

There are different ways to create app services. In the chapter, we will create our first app service using Azure Resource Manager (ARM). To get started, click "App Services" option in your dashboard.

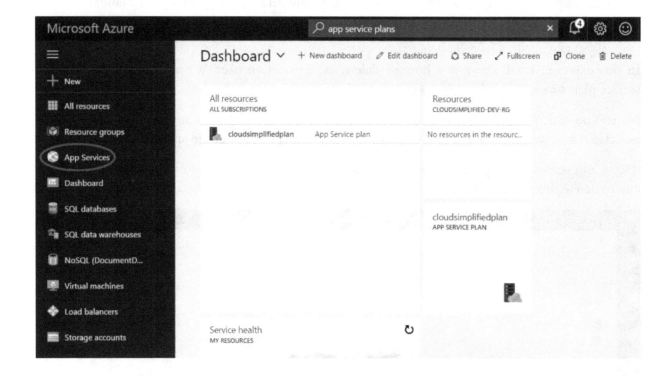

Then click on the "+Add" link.

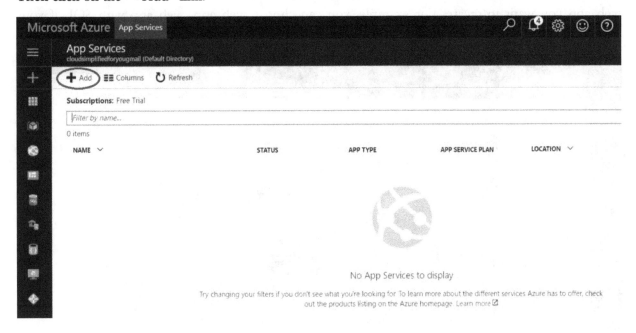

After you click "+Add" link you will be presented with a page that will allow you to choose type of web app you want to create. For example, you can choose web app, web app with SQL if your application needs to have a SQL database at back end. For our purpose, we will choose "Web App".

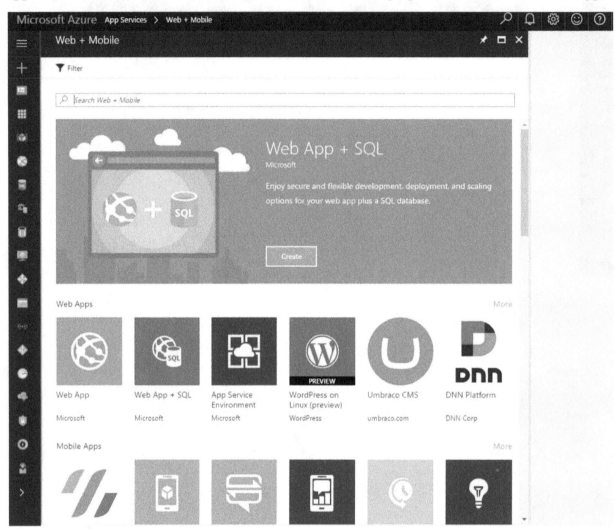

After you select web app, you will see the following page.

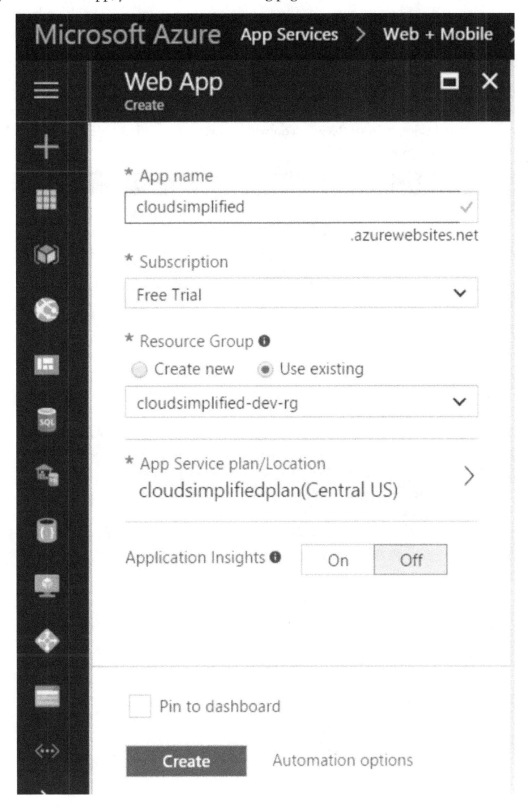

To create a web app, you need to enter app name, select subscription, create or use existing resource group, app service plan. For this exercise, I am going to enter name as "cloudsimplified", select resource group as "cloudsimplified-dev-rg".

Note: App name should be unique and no one else should be using it. You will get an error if app name is already in use.

If you have already created an app service plan, you can select it. Otherwise you can create a new app service plan by clicking "Create New". You will be presented with a "New App Service Plan" view on the right (see snapshot below).

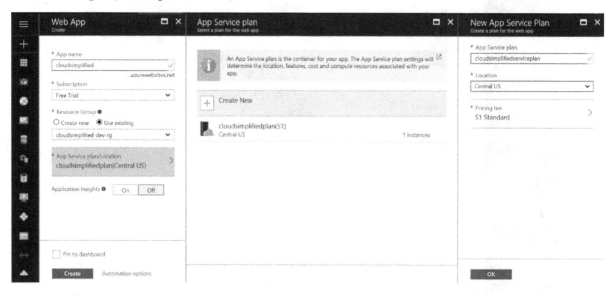

You will enter app service plan name, select location and pricing tier. For this exercise, I entered "cloudsimplifiedserviceplan" as app service plan and selected location as "Central US". To see all pricing tiers, click "Pricing Tier". You will be landed to the pricing web page where you can compare different pricing tiers and choose based on your requirements and usage.

Choose your pricing tier
Browse the available plans and their features

P1 Premium	P2 Premium	P3 Premium
1 Core	2 Core	4 Core
1.75 GB RAM	3.5 GB RAM	7 GB RAM
BizTalk Services	BizTalk Services	BizTalk Services
250 GB Storage	250 GB Storage	250 GB Storage
Up to 20 instances * Subject to availability	Up to 20 instances * Subject to availability	Up to 20 instances * Subject to availability
20 slots Web app staging	20 slots Web app staging	20 slots Web app staging
50 times daily Backup	50 times daily Backup	50 times daily Backup
Traffic Manager Geo availability	Traffic Manager Geo availability	Traffic Manager Geo availability
223.20 USD/MONTH (ESTIMATED)	**446.40** USD/MONTH (ESTIMATED)	**892.80** USD/MONTH (ESTIMATED)

S1 Standard	S2 Standard	S3 Standard
1 Core	2 Core	4 Core
1.75 GB RAM	3.5 GB RAM	7 GB RAM
50 GB Storage	50 GB Storage	50 GB Storage
Custom domains / SSL SNI Incl & IP SSL Support	Custom domains / SSL SNI Incl & IP SSL Support	Custom domains / SSL SNI Incl & IP SSL Support
Up to 10 instances Auto scale	Up to 10 instances Auto scale	Up to 10 instances Auto scale
Daily Backup	Daily Backup	Daily Backup
5 slots Web app staging	5 slots Web app staging	5 slots Web app staging
Traffic Manager Geo availability	Traffic Manager Geo availability	Traffic Manager Geo availability
44.64 USD/MONTH (ESTIMATED)	**89.28** USD/MONTH (ESTIMATED)	**178.56** USD/MONTH (ESTIMATED)

B1 Basic	B2 Basic	B3 Basic
1 Core	2 Core	4 Core

Select

19

As you can see from above snapshot, different plan provides different set of resources. For example, in premium pricing tier we can have up to 20 instances, while in standard pricing tier we can have up to 10 instances. As expected, more you are willing to pay, more resources you can get.

You can select pricing tier and click on the "Create" button to create Web App. Once your web app is created you can see it on your account homepage, under all resources. Also, as shown below you will get a notification from Azure once web app creation is complete. To see the notification, click on the bell icon.

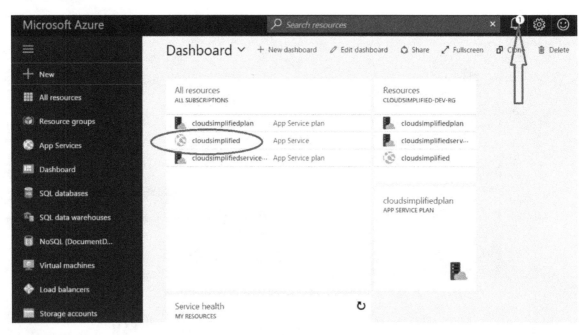

Now click on this newly created app service ("cloudsimplified" in our case). You will be presented with following page.

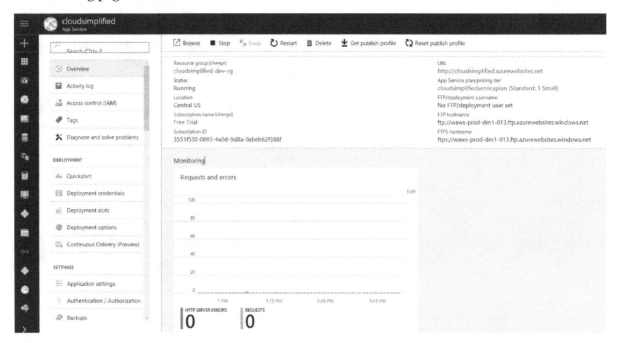

We will explore these options later in the book. As seen on the above snapshot, you now have a URL for your app. You can click on this URL to browse to your web application.

Chapter Three: Deployment Slots

What are Deployment Slots

The idea behind development slots is that you can have multiple instances of your web application. Each deployment slot represents separate instance of web app. Default slot is called "production". If you create a new web application and deploy it, by default it will go to production slot. In the previous chapter, we created our first web app. We also looked at the URL for web app. Since we did not explicitly create any slot, our web app was deployed to production slot. One important thing to remember is you can only create slots when running web app in standard or premium pricing tier.

Incremental and Staged Deployments

Slots can be used to do incremental and staged deployments. Let us say you have created two slots (Dev and QA) for your application. You make some changes to your application and deploy it to Dev slot. Then developers will do some testing and once they feel they are done with their testing they can move it to QA slot. Once it is in QA, QA team can run automated test and once everything looks good, code can be moved to production slot. One important point to note here is all slots will run on same virtual machine using same hardware.

Exercise 4: Create a new Deployment Slot

Under app service dashboard you can see a link for "Deployment slots". Click on it and then click on the "+Add slot" link.

After you click "+Add slot" you will be presented with following page.

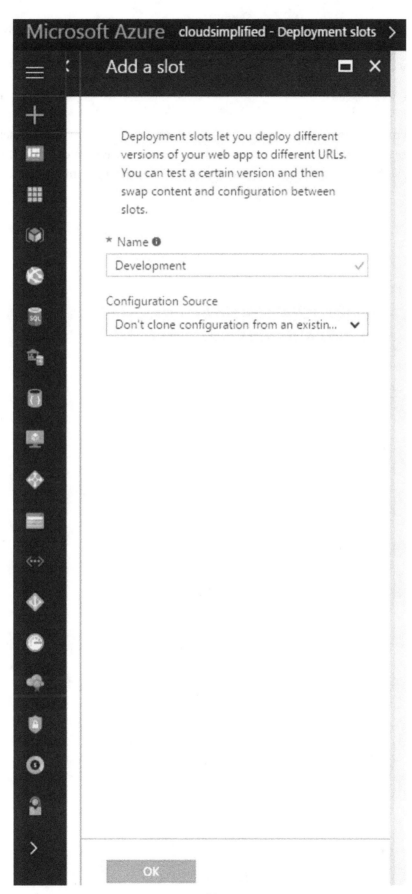

To create a slot, you need to enter name. Let us call it "Development" for our exercise. Then you can select the configuration source. You can clone all configuration settings from an existing slot. For our exercise, we will choose "Don't clone configuration" settings. Click on the "OK" button to create a slot.

Number of Deployment Slots

Number of deployment slots you can have depends on app service plan you have selected. Standard Tier provides 5 slots and Premium Tier 20 slots. Each slot will have its own URL for web app. As mentioned earlier, slots can be used to do incremental and staged deployments.

Chapter Four: Deploy Web Apps using Visual Studio

In chapter 2, we created a web app using portal and deployed it. While deploying, we did not specify any information about slot we are deploying to. So, our app was deployed to default slot (production slot). In this chapter, we will create a new MVC application using Visual Studio and publish it to a "Development" slot that we created earlier. To create a new ASP.NET application using Visual Studio, click on File→New Project and select ASP.NET Web application. Give a name to your new application.

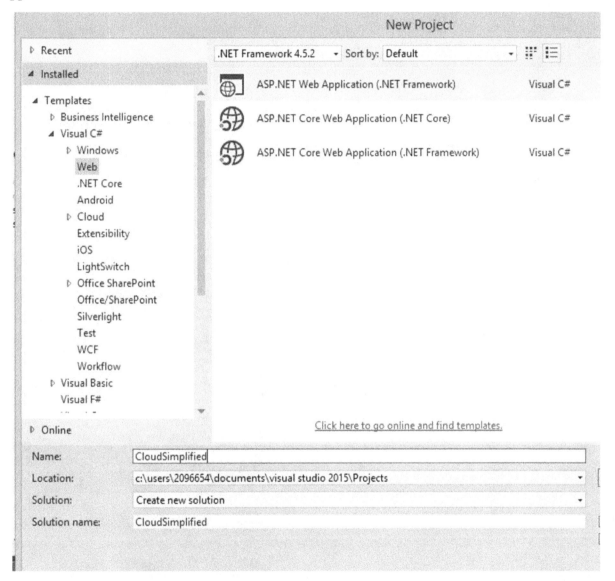

Then click on the "OK" button to go to next screen.

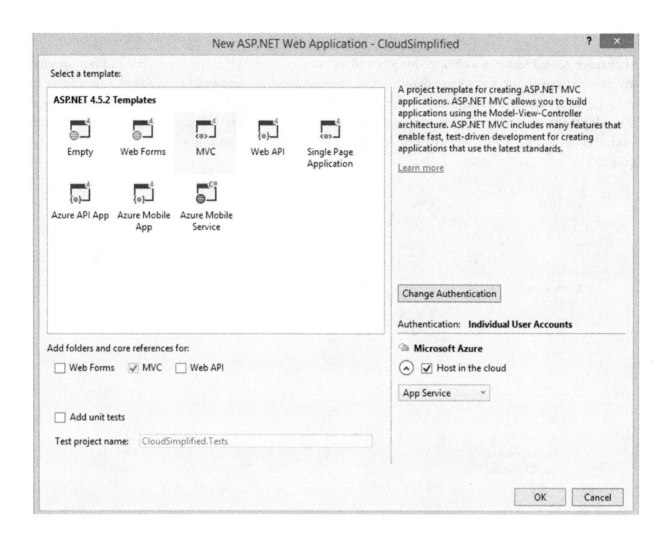

Select MVC and click "Change Authentication".

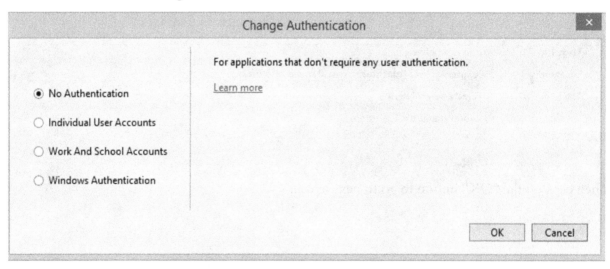

Select "No Authentication" radio button and then click on the "OK" Button.

Now enter the app name in the "Web App Name" textbox, select your subscription, select or create a resource group and app service plan. For this exercise, "cloudsimplified-dev-rg" as a resource group and "cloudsimplifiedserviceplan" as our app service plan. Then click on the "Create" button.

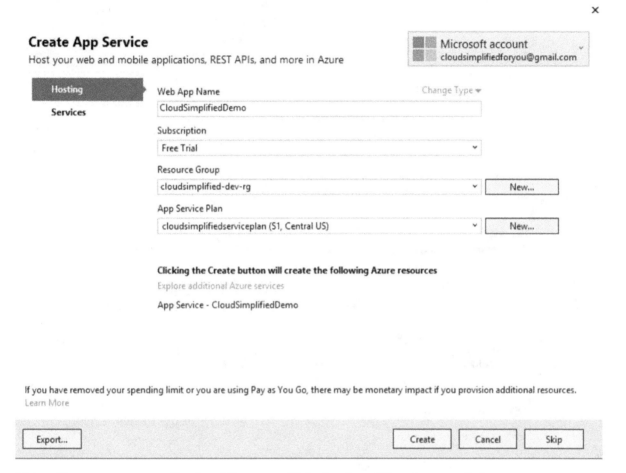

This will create a new application. Now we will deploy it to "Development" slot.

Right click on the project and click "Publish".

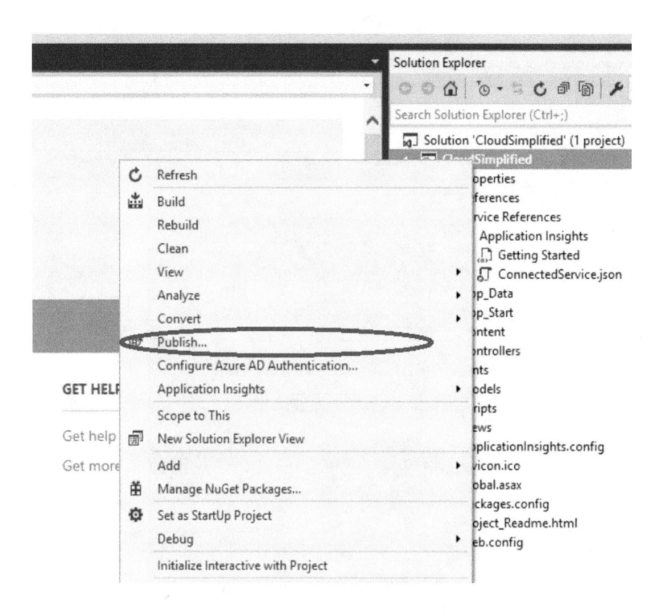

Select Microsoft Azure App service.

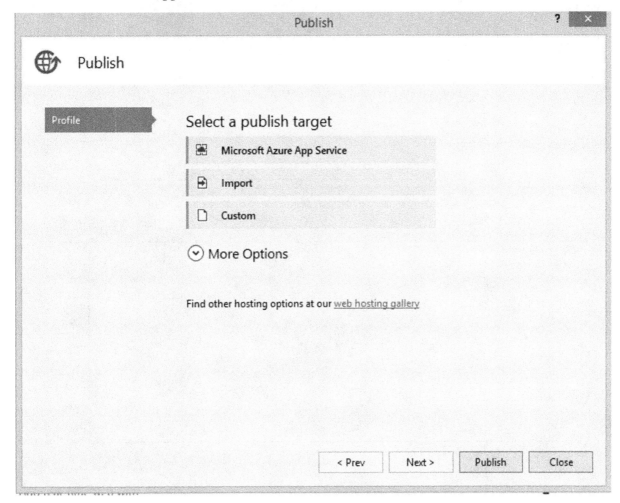

Now select subscription. Then expand resource group and select "Development" slot. Click on the "Ok" button.

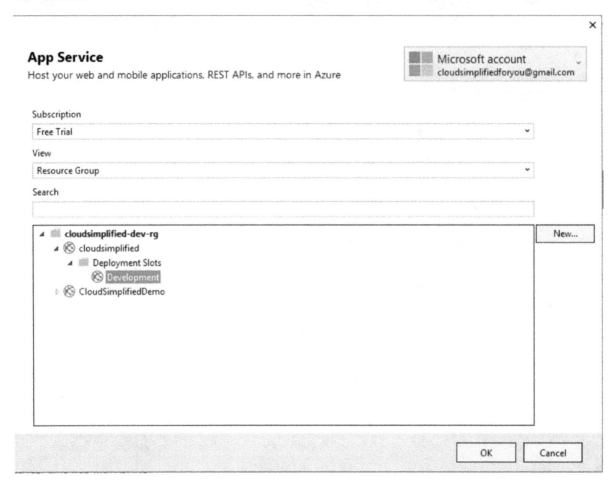

You will be presented with the screen as shown on the next page. On the "Connection" tab choose publish method as "Web Deploy".

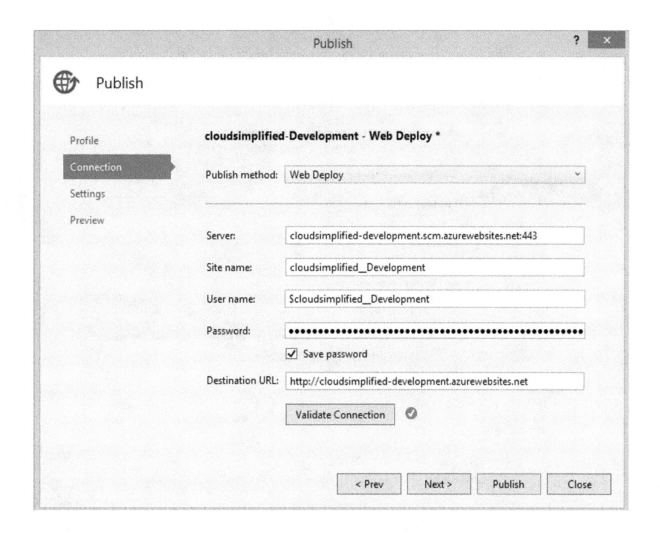

Then click on the "Settings" link. Here you can select configuration. You can choose either "Release" or "Debug". If you are troubleshooting any issue and want to remote debug your application, then choose "Debug" as Configuration. For our exercise, we will choose "Release".

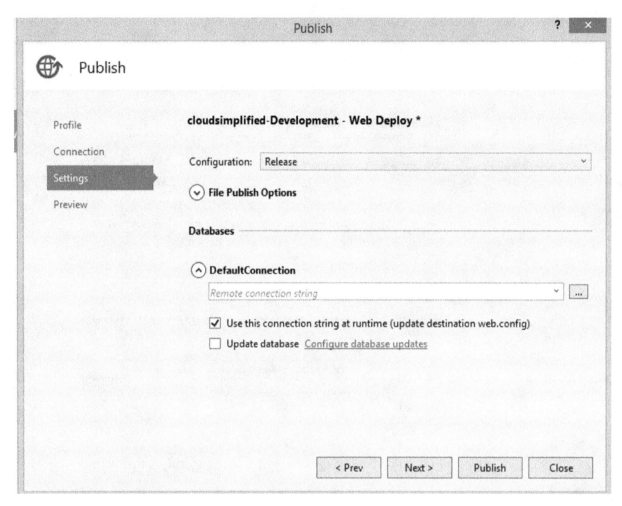

Click on the "Publish" button. You can check status of deployment in the output window. Once it is published, you should be able to see publish succeed message. See snapshot below to see what to expect in the output window.

```
Output
Show output from: Build                                         ▼  | ⏸ | ⏹ ⏺ | ⏫ | ⏩
2>Adding file (cloudsimplified__Development\Scripts\bootstrap.js).
2>Adding file (cloudsimplified__Development\Scripts\bootstrap.min.js).
2>Adding file (cloudsimplified__Development\Scripts\jquery-1.10.2.js).
2>Adding file (cloudsimplified__Development\Scripts\jquery-1.10.2.min.js).
2>Adding file (cloudsimplified__Development\Scripts\jquery-1.10.2.min.map).
2>Adding file (cloudsimplified__Development\Scripts\jquery.validate.js).
2>Adding file (cloudsimplified__Development\Scripts\jquery.validate.min.js).
2>Adding file (cloudsimplified__Development\Scripts\jquery.validate.unobtrusive.js).
2>Adding file (cloudsimplified__Development\Scripts\jquery.validate.unobtrusive.min.js).
2>Adding file (cloudsimplified__Development\Scripts\modernizr-2.6.2.js).
2>Adding file (cloudsimplified__Development\Scripts\respond.js).
2>Adding file (cloudsimplified__Development\Scripts\respond.min.js).
2>Adding file (cloudsimplified__Development\Scripts\_references.js).
2>Adding file (cloudsimplified__Development\Service References\Application Insights\ConnectedService.json).
2>Adding file (cloudsimplified__Development\Views\Home\About.cshtml).
2>Adding file (cloudsimplified__Development\Views\Home\Contact.cshtml).
2>Adding file (cloudsimplified__Development\Views\Home\Index.cshtml).
2>Adding file (cloudsimplified__Development\Views\Shared\Error.cshtml).
2>Adding file (cloudsimplified__Development\Views\Shared\_Layout.cshtml).
2>Adding file (cloudsimplified__Development\Views\Web.config).
2>Adding file (cloudsimplified__Development\Views\_ViewStart.cshtml).
2>Adding file (cloudsimplified__Development\Web.config).
2>Adding ACL's for path (cloudsimplified__Development)
2>Adding ACL's for path (cloudsimplified__Development)
2>Publish Succeeded.
2>Web App was published successfully http://cloudsimplified-development.azurewebsites.net/
========== Build: 1 succeeded, 0 failed, 0 up-to-date, 0 skipped ==========
========== Publish: 1 succeeded, 0 failed, 0 skipped ==========
```

For this exercise, we selected web deploy as publish method. One of the other option we have for publish method is "Web Deploy Package". If you choose this option, then you can create a package (zip folder with all information required to deploy web app to Azure) and save this package on computer. Then you can use PowerShell command to deploy this package in cloud. In the chapter on PowerShell I have shown how you can use PowerShell commands to create or update your web app using a package.

Note: In the real world, you will have different versions of same application in different slots. For us to be able to easily see difference visually, I have deployed two different applications on two different slots.

As mentioned earlier, each slot represents an instance of web app. Click "cloudsimplified" resource under all resources.

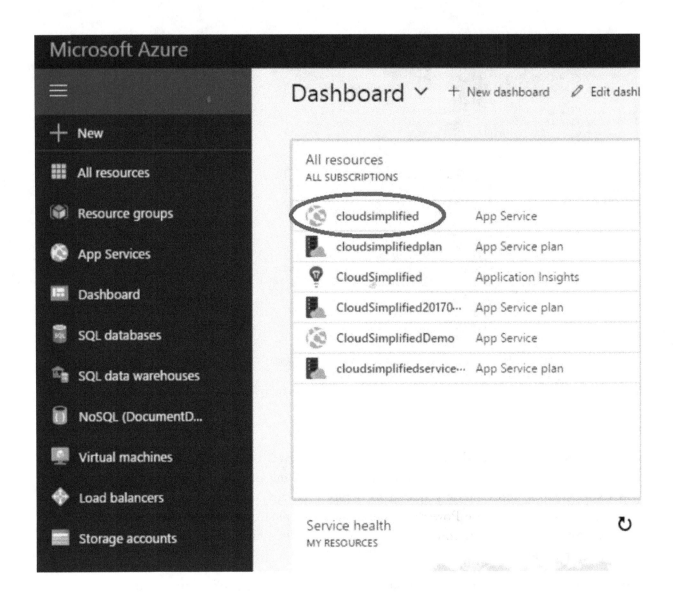

Then click "Deployment slots" on the dashboard. On the right side, it will start showing all the slots available for cloudsimplified web app (see snapshot below). Click on the "cloudsimplified-development" slot.

After you click, you can see a page with details about the slot.

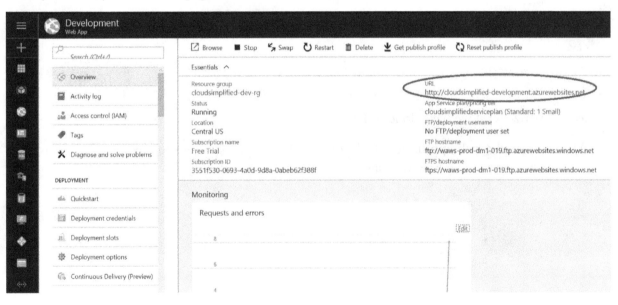

Copy the URL and paste it in your web browser. Great work, you have deployed your web app to the development slot.

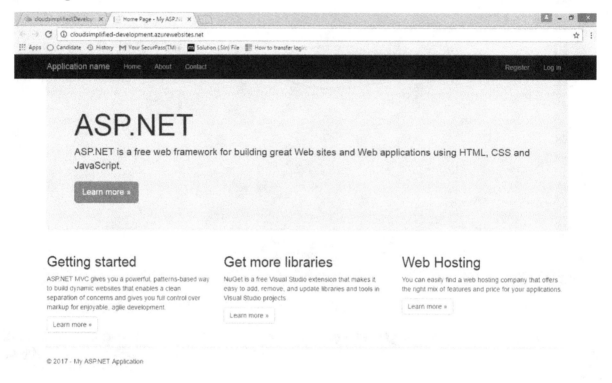

So, to summarize what we have done so far:

A) We created a web app using ARM portal and deployed it to production slot. Just to refresh your memory this is how website looks in production slot.

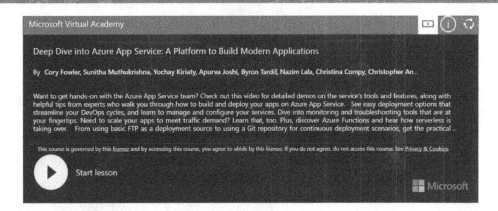

B) Then we created a deployment slot. We named it "Development".

C) After that we created a new web app using Visual Studio and deployed it to "Development" slot. See snapshot on page 36 to see how website looks in development slot.

D) Like I said before, in the real world, you will have different versions of same application in different slots. Just for our convenience, I deployed two different applications in Dev and Production slot.

Swapping Deployment Slots

Swapping means moving code from one slot to another slot (example from Dev to QA slot).

Note: All slots are on same virtual machine, if we continuously swap slots, it can have some impact on production web app.

We can also set slots to swap automatically. This is called auto swap. What it means is whenever we deploy to one slot say dev for example, it will automatically get swapped with another slot say QA Slot.

Swap with preview – an option that gives us the most control over the swap process. It allows us to fully verify the new version of app before it is swapped into production.

Exercise 5: Swap Slots

In chapter two of this book, we deployed our application to production slot. Then in chapter 4, we created another application using Visual Studio and deployed it to development slot. Now we are going to swap development and production slots. After swapping is complete, we can expect production website to have content from dev website and vice a versa.

To do swapping, go to web app and click "Deployment slots".

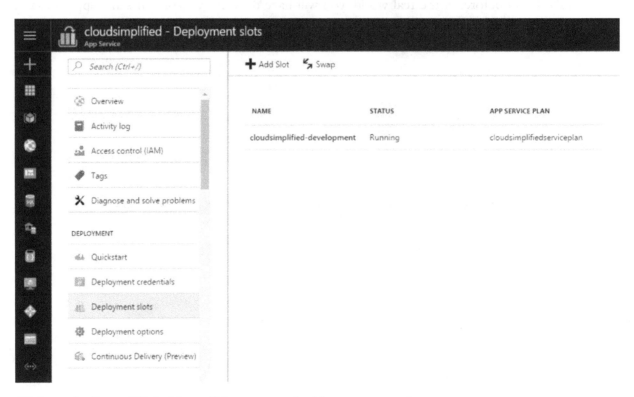

Click on the "swap" link. You will be presented with a screen as shown on next page.

Note: There are different ways to swap slots.

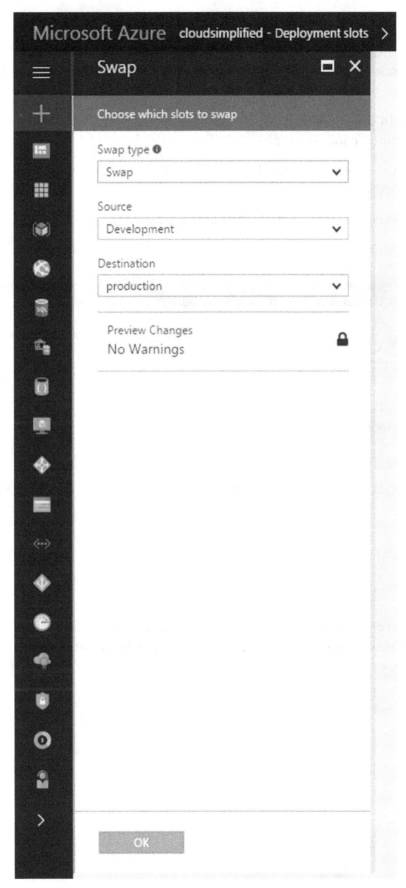

Swap Type: This drop down has two values: swap and swap with preview. For our exercise, we will select Swap.

Source: We can see all slots in this dropdown. We will select our source slot in this dropdown. In our case, it will be "Development".

Destination: In this dropdown, we can also see all our slots. Remember production slot is always there by default. We will select "production" as destination slot.

Ok Button: One you have selected swap type, source slot and destination slot, click on the "Ok" button to swap.

Once swapping is complete go to Production URL.

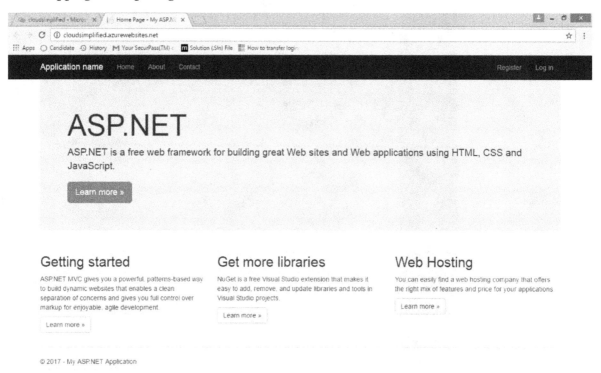

As we can see from above snapshot, production URL now has content that was in dev site. Similarly, browse to dev URL and you will see that it has content from production website (See snapshot below).

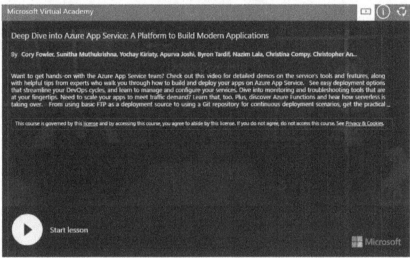

Roll back a Deployment

Every once in a while, your deployment will have some issues. It could be a permission issue or you may find some critical bugs after you have deployed your website into production. In these circumstances, you must do a roll back. Using deployment slots, you can easily rollback your changes by doing another swap with production slot.

Chapter Five: App Service Plans

App Service plans represent the collection of physical resources used to host your apps. Apps in the same subscription, region, and resource group can share an App Service plan. All applications assigned to an App Service plan share the resources defined by it, allowing you to save cost when hosting multiple apps in a single App Service plan.

Scale Up

Scale up means changing the app service plan pricing tier and instance size. Any change made to an app service plan will apply to all web apps in that plan. To Scale up, click on "Scale up (App Service plan)" option under Settings.

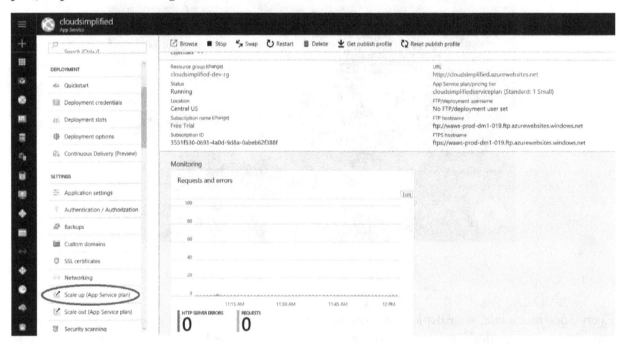

After you click "Scale up (App Service plan)" you will be presented with following page.

You can select the pricing tier you want.

Note: Azure won't allow you to lower your service plan if you are using some features that are in higher plan but not in lower plan.

Scale Out

Scale out means increasing the number of VM instances that run your app. You can scale out to as many as 50 instances, depending on your pricing tier. To scale out, click on the "Scale out (App Service plan)" option. Just like scale up, any change made to an app service plan for scaling out will apply to all web aps under that plan.

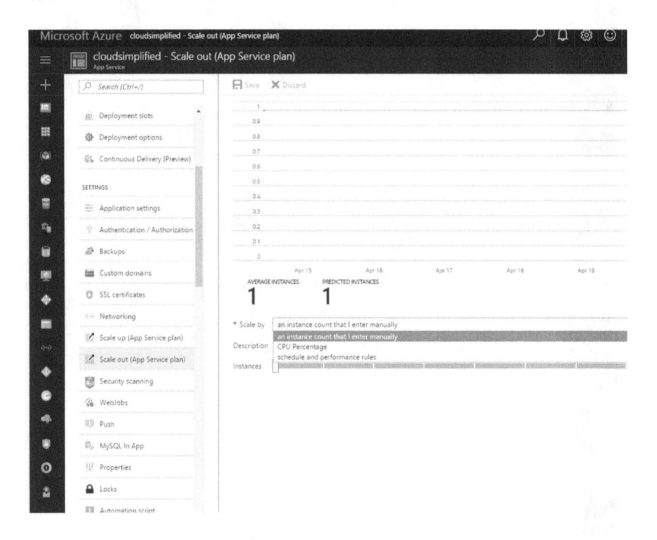

Scale out can be done in the following three different ways.

Scale Out by Instance Count

You can Scale out by an instance count entered manually. It means you will define number of instances you need. Example: let us say you created a new web site and demand is low to begin with. You can set instance count as 1. As demand increases for your website you can come into portal and change instance count to 2 or higher number.

Scale Out by CPU Percentage

Second option to scale out is by CPU percentage. When you select this option, you will be asked to enter range of instances and range of CPU percentage. Let us say you set range of instances from 3 to 6 and range of CPU from 30% to 80%. What it means is minimum number of instances you want is 3 and maximum 6. So, you will start with 3 instances. If CPU percentage goes up to more than 80 percentage, another instance will be added automatically. If total number of instances is less than or equal to 6, Azure will keep on adding instances assuming CPU percentage stays above 80. As you add more instances, CPU percentage will likely come down. If CPU percentage goes below 30%, Azure will start removing instances. It means that it will automatically scale down if CPU percentage is less than lower range of threshold value you have set. As Azure automatically scales up or scale down, you can set up notifications by entering email addresses in the Additional Email(s) textbox or by checking Email Administrators and Co-Administrators Check Box.

Scale Out by Schedule and Performance Rules.

Third option to scale out is by schedule and performance rules. This options gives more flexibility than the other two options. When you choose this option, you can create a profile and add rules. You can set up rules to increase or decrease instances based on certain conditions.

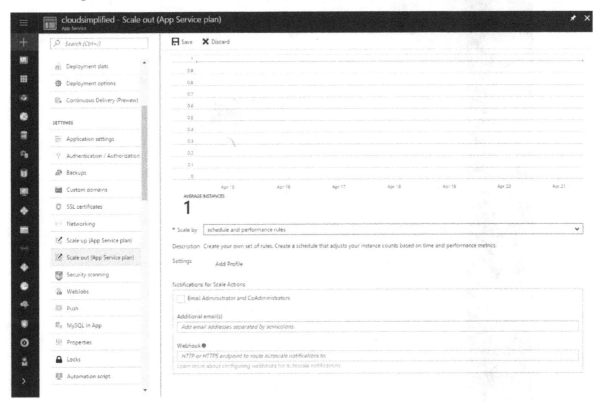

Click on the "Add Profile" link. It will open a new Page with "Scale profile" as title.

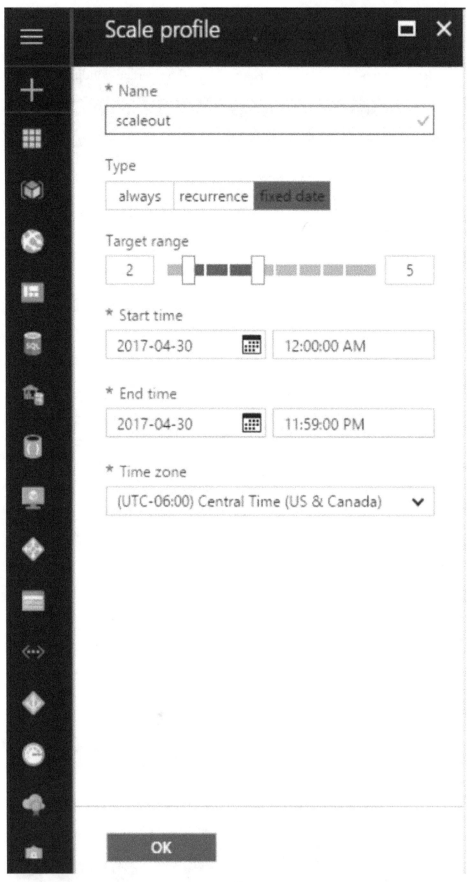

As you can see from the above snapshot you need to give a name to the profile. Then you need to choose type. Type can be one of the following: always, recurrence or fixed date. If you know you web app will get lot of traffic during certain fixed days in a year, then you can choose type as "fixed date" and set it up to have more instances on those days. One the other hand if you know you web app traffic patterns and you see that on every Sunday you are getting lot of traffic, then you can choose "recurrence" as a type.

Once you select all your settings you can click on the "Ok" button to create a profile.

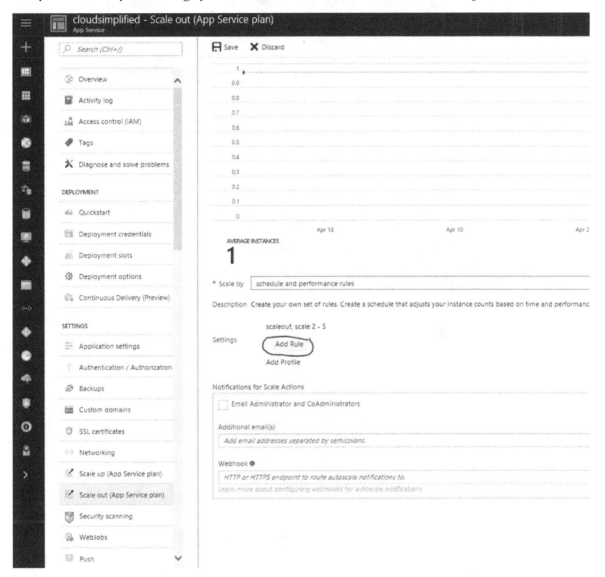

Now that you have created a profile, you can add rules to it. Rules are used to set up conditions for scaling up or down. Click on the "Add Rule" link to start creating a rule.

Let us say you want instance count to go up by 1 when CPU percentage is more than 80% and decrease by 1 when CPU percent goes below 30 %. To achieve this, you can create two rules. One for incrementing instances and other for decrementing them. When we set up rules we can also define duration and cool down period. Duration is how long it should wait to create an instance after CPU percentage has gone more than threshold (80% in our example) value. We do not want to create a new instance every time CPU percentage goes more than the threshold value. It could just be a momentary spike. We want to wait for few minutes and make sure we do have some real continuous traffic that keeps CPU percentage more than the threshold value. This is what duration does.

Cool down on the other hand is how long it should wait to scale up or down again after the previous scale.

While setting up rules you choose the action you want to take. Options are:

- Increase or decrease by - Choose this option if you want to add or remove instances.
- Increase or decrease percent – Choose this option if you want to change the instance count by a percent.
- Increase or decrease to - this will set the instance count to the value you define.

Next snapshot shows all the options that are in the "Action" dropdown menu.

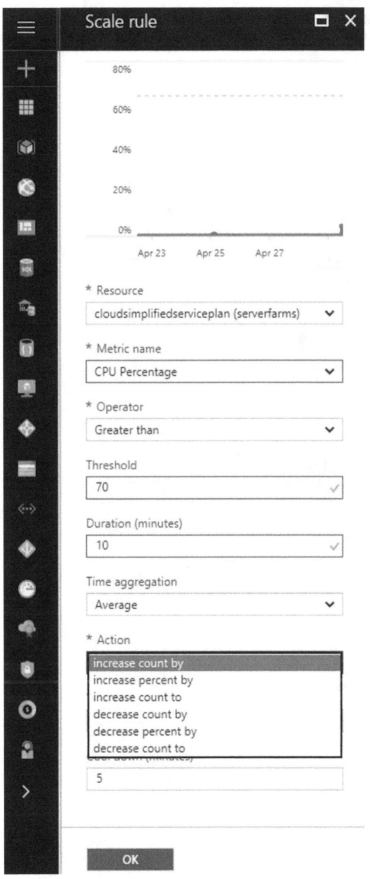

Also, while creating a rule you must choose a metric. For our example, we have chosen "CPU Percentage" as a metric. See the snapshot below for all options available under "Metric name" dropdown.

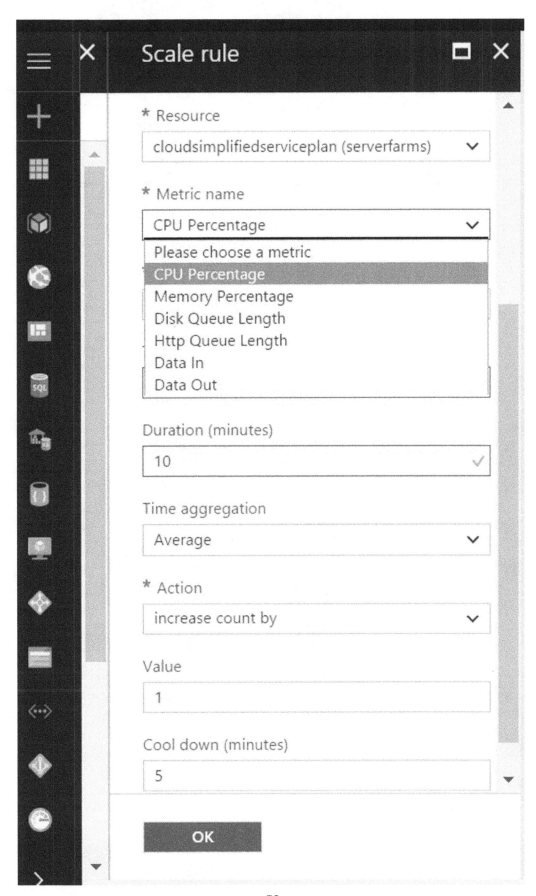

Example: Create a rule for reducing instance count by 1 when CPU Percentage goes below 30%.

Choose "CPU Percentage" as a metric name, "decrease count by" as Action. Set other values as shown or as desired.

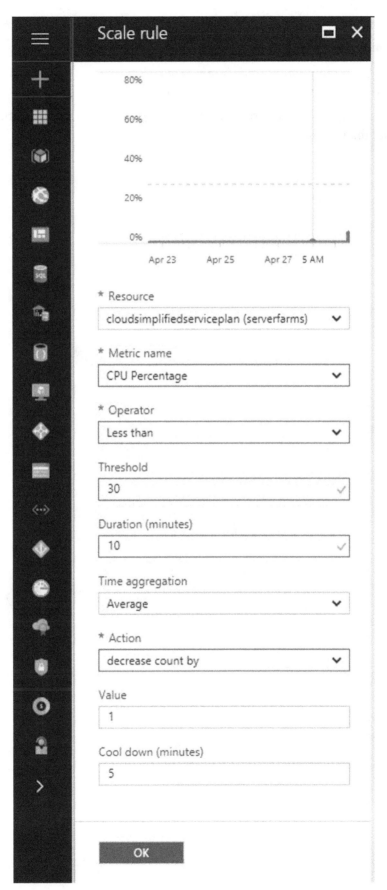

Example: Rule for increasing instance count by 1 when CPU Percentage goes above 70% and stays above 70% for more than 10 minutes.

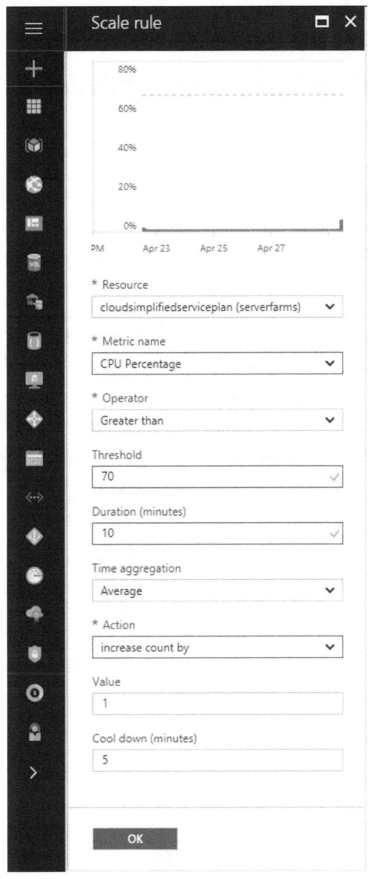

Change App Service Plan for a Web App

We can change the app service plan for a web app. Click on the "Change App Service plan" link under App Service plan.

Note: if you try to scale down to a lower pricing tier, and if you are using some of the features of higher pricing tier, Azure won't let you scale down.

Chapter Six: App Service Settings

In this chapter we will look at how to set application settings using ARM portal. To get started, go to your web app and click on the "Application settings" link. After you click, you will see a page with general settings, debugging settings, app settings, connection settings and handler mappings.

- General Settings: Framework Versions: Here you can set framework versions of .NET, PHP,Java or Python. If your webapp is using any of these you can come here and set version information.

- Platform: Depending on whether your application is 32 bit or 64 bit, you can set the setting here.

- Web Sockets: You can set web sockets to on to enable web socket protocol.

- Always On: To conserve resources, web Apps are unloaded if they are idle for some period of time. If you want to keep the application loaded at all time you can set Always On setting to On.

- Managed Pipeline Version: This setting sets the IIS pipeline mode.

- Auto Swap: As discussed earlier this setting is used to automatically do the swapping between slots.

- Remote Debugging: You can enable this setting if you want to debug your application.
  Note: for remote debugging to work, you must deploy debug version of your application.

- App Settings: If you are using .NET application, app settings can be defined in app.config. However, if you define the same setting in portal, then the value in portal will override the value defined in app.config file. Another important thing to note here is that we have a "slot setting" checkbox in front of each app or connection setting (see snapshot below). If this checkbox is check, this app setting won't get swapped when we do a swapping between slots. This is useful when you have a setting that is specific to the environment. For example, folder path in dev may be different from folder path in Production. So, when we swap production and dev slot we do not want to swap folder path setting.

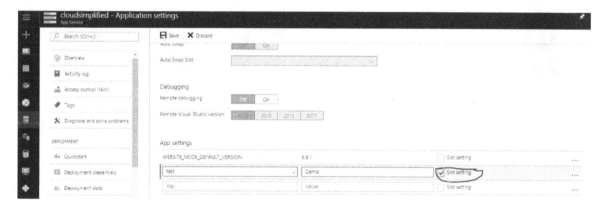

- Connection Settings: We can define our connection settings here.
- Default Documents: default document is a web page displayed at root level for web app.

- Handler Mappings: Let us say you are using an older version of PHP. This version is not by default in Azure. You can use handler mappings to define type of file (example:.php), path of Script processor and any additional arguments that processor may need.

Next two snapshots show all the application settings that can be configured in ARM portal.

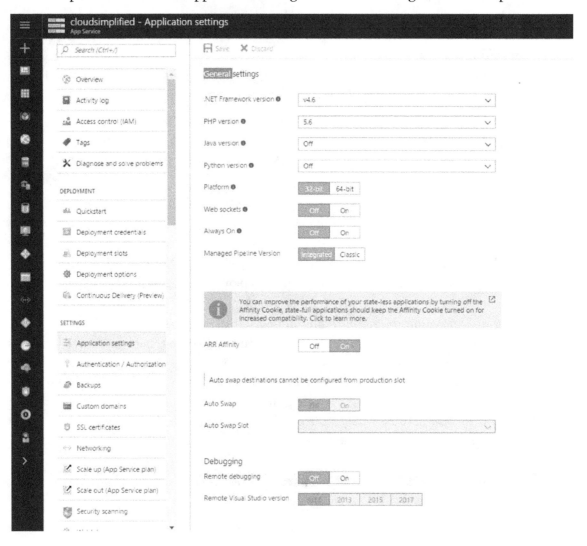

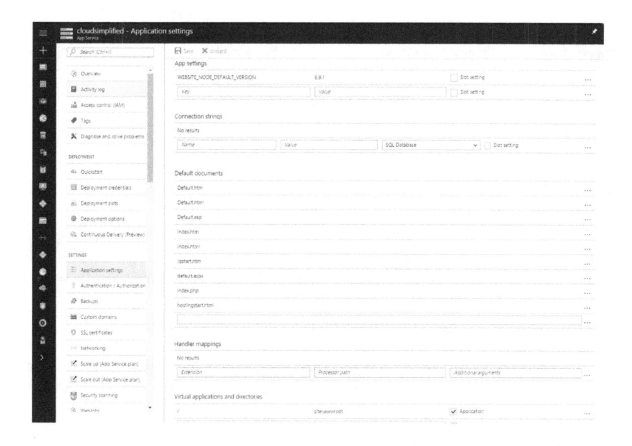

App settings can be defined in configuration file or in ARM portal (under Application Settings). To access settings in the configuration file using .NET we can use following code:

Code: System.Configuration.Manager.AppSettings["Setting1"]

To access settings in ARM portal we can use

Code: @Environment.GetEnvironmentVariable(AppSetting_Setting1]

Note: If you have same setting in app.config and ARM portal, value of setting in ARM portal will be used.

Custom domain

By default, when we create a web app in Azure we get site address as SiteName.Azurewebsites.net. In the real world, we may not want website to stay on shared domain AzureWebsites.net, instead we may want our website to have URL like SiteName.com.

To achieve this what we can do is buy a domain (example "SiteName.com") and then add a DNS record of Type "A" (Host to IP map) or Type CNAME in domain. "A" record is like www.SiteName.com should go to Azure IP address 40.74.253.108. CNAME on the other hand maps custom domain to Azure Doman. CNAME will persist even when IP address of VM changes. For "A" type record you can get Azure IP address from External IP address section in Custom Domains (See snapshot on next page). If you add Type "A" record you will have to add additional TXT record. This record will help you to validate in the ARM portal. On the other hand, if you add CNAME record you do not need to enter additional TXT record.

Example of "A" Record

Fully Qualified Domain Name	A Host	A Value
SiteName.com	@	40.74.253.108

Example of TXT Record

Fully Qualified Domain Name	A Host	A Value
SiteName.com	@	Cloudsimplified.azurewebsites.net

Example of CNAME Record

Fully Qualified Domain Name	A Host	A Value
www.SiteName.com	www	Cloudsimplified.azurewebsites.net

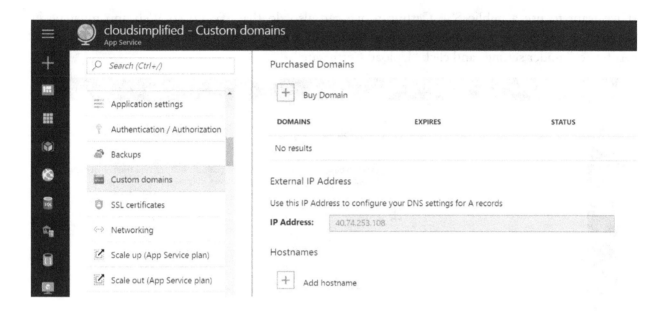

Last step in setting up custom domain is to Validate. Click "Add hostname", enter your fully qualified domain name (Example: www.SiteName.com") and validate.

Note: Free Tier app service plan does not allow custom domains.

SSL Settings

We have seen that when we deploy websites in Azure, they are part of Azurewebsites.net shared domain by default. What is very interesting is, if you put HTTPS in the URL for your website, it will still work and you will see a lock symbol and secured connection (see snapshot below).

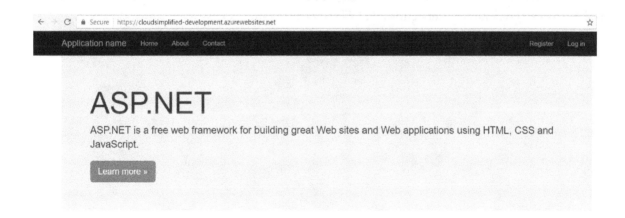

By default, Azure supports SSL. Microsoft certificate is in trusted root certification authority store on most if not all computers in the world.

If we want to use a public SSL Certificate we can also do that. To do so Web app must be in standard or premium domain. First step is to upload a certificate in the SSL portal. Go to "SSL certificates" under settings and click "Upload Certificate".

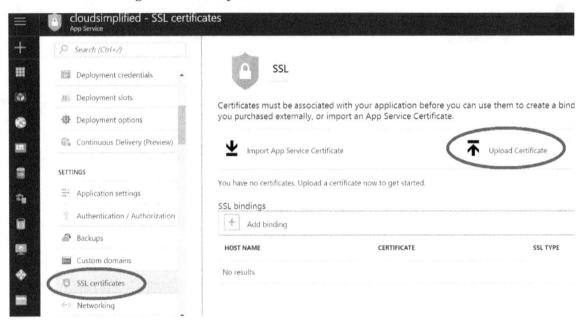

It will ask for path for PFX Certificate File and password as shown in snapshot on next page. After you have selected path for certificate file and entered password, click on the "Upload" button to upload a certificate. Once certificate has been uploaded we can get its thumbprint from the portal. This thumbprint must match to the thumbprint value in web.config. If you want your website to be accessible from HTTP and HTTPS then configuration is complete. However, if you do not want your app to be accessible from HTTP, then you need to enforce HTTPS on your app. To do so you will have to define a rewrite rule in web.config. This rewrite rule should do a permanent redirect to HTTPS protocol whenever user sends a HTTP request.

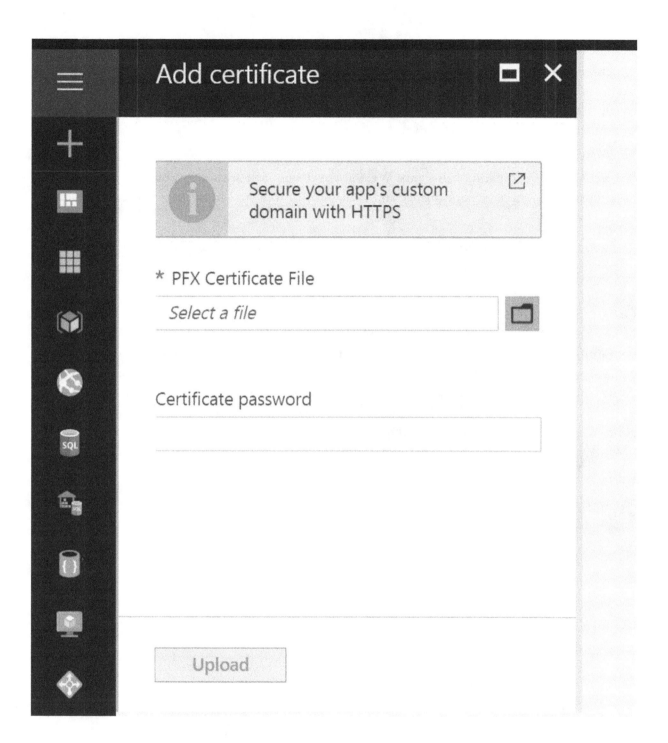

Chapter Seven: Logs and Monitoring

A website is only good as its content and response time. If your web app is slow, then you will most likely end up losing some of your users. As important it is to design your web application, it is equally important to monitor it. In this chapter, we will go through different ways to monitor your web app.

Application Insights:

We will start with Application Insights. We will cover only few areas of Application Insights. It is basically a way to monitor performance and availability of web app. It can help in diagnosing quality issues in web apps.

The good thing is that application insight is integrated with Visual Studio. You can use Application insight to query logs/data created by web app.

End Point Monitoring

One of the topics we will cover under application insights is End Point monitoring. Let us say you have a web app which will be consumed by users in different parts of the world. As a website owner, you want to make sure that users, irrespective of their geographical location can load your website without too much response time. This is where Availability test can help. We can create a Availability test, configure it by choosing up to five locations from where we can constantly ping our web app. We can create an alert if ping fails for one or more locations. In the next exercise, we will see how we can create Availability Tests through portal.

Exercise 6: Create Availability Tests
  1) Click "Application Insights" under monitoring.

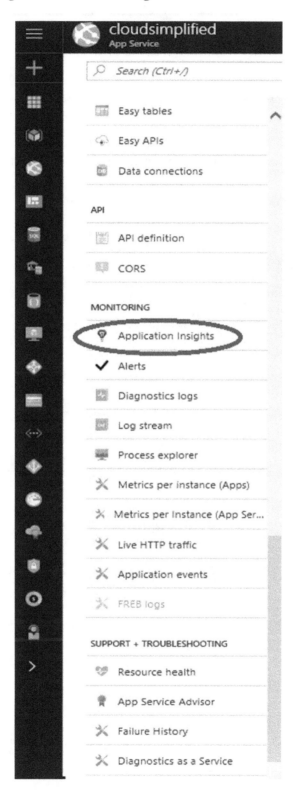

2) Click "View More in Application Insights". If you are doing it for first time, then you will be asked to select a resource group.

 Application Insights

Application Insights helps you detect and diagnose quality issues in your web apps and web services, and helps you understand what your users actually do with it. Learn more

This App Service is associated with the Application Insights resource: **CloudSimplified** (change)

Slowest Requests (past 24 hours)

REQUEST NAME	DURATION (95TH)
GET Home/Index	3.78 sec
GET /	0.0 ms

Live Stream

```
5                                          ▌ REQUESTS
4
3
2
1
0
5                                          ▌ FAILURES
4
3
2
1
0
100ms                                      ▌ DURATION
80ms
60ms
40ms
20ms
0ms
    -60s.                                       0s.
```

VIEW MORE IN APPLICATION INSIGHTS

3) After you click on View more in Application Insights, you will see a page like shown below.

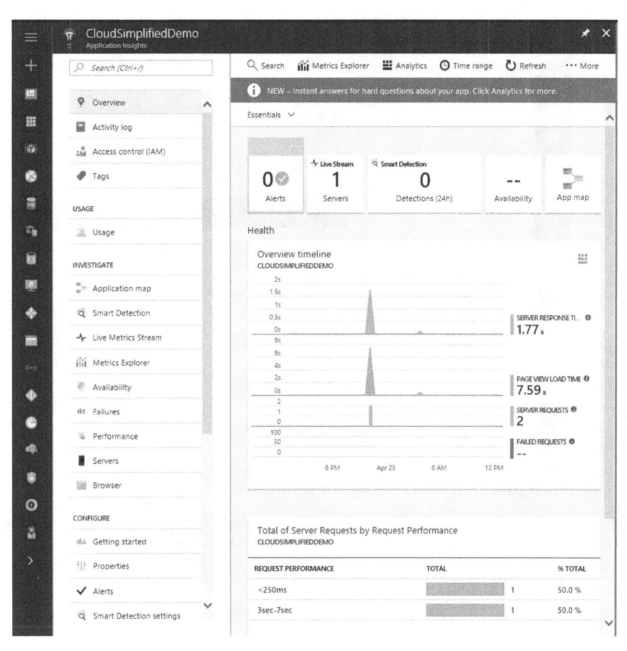

4) Availability Test –You can click on "Availability" under Investigate. Then click on "Add test" link.

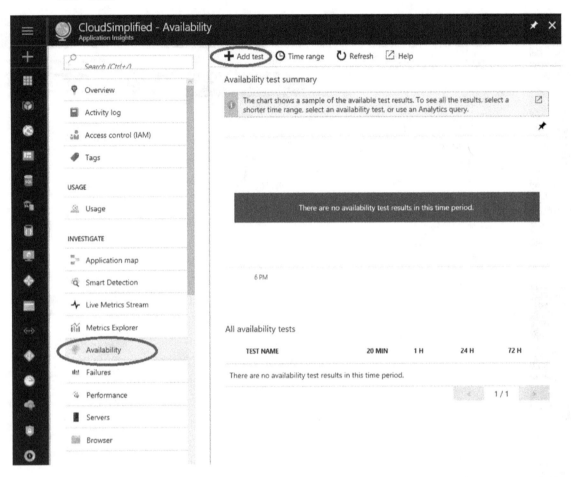

5) After you click "Add test", you will see a page where you can configure your app for availability test. What that means is you can select up to 5 locations, duration and success criteria. You can also set up alerts and get notified whenever certain conditions are not met. After you enter all values, you can click on the "Create" button to create Availability Test.

* Test name

[   ]

Test type

[URL ping test   ⌄]

* URL ❶

[http://CloudSimplifiedDemo.azurewebsites.net]

Parse dependent requests ❶

[✓]

Enable retries for availability test failures. ❶

[✓]

Test frequency ❶

[5 minutes   ⌄]

Test locations ❶   ❯
5 location(s) configured

Success criteria ❶   ❯
HTTP response: 200, Test Timeou...

Alerts ●   ❯
Alert if 3/5 locations fails in 5 mi...

[Create]

Telemetry

Telemetry is collecting data from remote machines or inaccessible end points and transmitting them. VM's on which web apps run are not accessible directly. So, to monitor them we use telemetry.

Metrics

Metrics are data points for your app. They are available from basic tier and higher. Example: number of requests, average response time, number of HTTP errors.

Alerts

Alerts are rules such that when a condition that you are monitoring reaches above or below a threshold value that you have set, you can get an email. Through ARM you can create alerts for your web app. They can be on metrics or events (like start, stop)

Let us see how to create an alert. First click on "Alerts" under monitoring. Then click on the "Add alert" link.

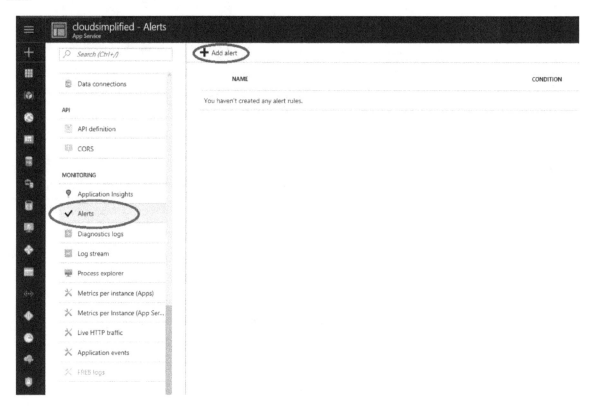

After you click "Add alert", you will be presented with an alert rule page. On this page, you can configure rules, threshold values and emails. Example: If you want to create an alert and get notified when number of HTTP 403 errors exceeds 10 in the last 30 minutes, you can choose alert on "metrics", and "Http 403" as metric, condition as "Greater than", threshold value as 10 and period as "Over the last 30 minutes". You can also enter email ids of people you want to alert.

When we use PAAS we do not have direct access to VM's on which web app is running. However, we do have access to various log sources. Let us first see what log sources we have:

1) Event log (Format: XML)

2) IIS Web server logs –W3C extened log file format(delimited file format)
   Path on VM: D:\home\LogFiles\Http\RawLogs

3) Detailed error message logs (http 400 and higher)
   Path on VM: D:\home\LogFiles\DetailedErrors

4) Freb Logs (detailed xml info, one file per traced request)
   Path on VM: D:\home\LogFiles\W3svc<random#>

5) App diagnostic logs: We can also Add code in .net to log messages .
   Example Trace.TraceWarning("Test").
   Path: D:\home\LogFiles\Application

We can enable diagnostic logs from ARM portal, Visual Studio server explorer, Powershell. We can pull these logs through ftp, portal, site control manager (kudu), Visual studio server explorer, PowerShell.

Diagnostic logs

Click "Diagnostics logs" under monitoring. You will be presented with a page similar to what I have shown below. Again, I say similar because Azure team is doing continous development.

Note: By default all logging settings are turned off.

App diagnostic logs can be stored in file system or in blob. First setting "Application Logging(Filesystem)" when set to "On" will log in files. Second setting on the page is "Application Logging (Blob) ". This setting when set to "On" will store app logs in blob. You can also enable web server logging, detailed error messages logging and failed request tracing from this page.

Note: To store in blob you need to have a storage account.

At the bottom of the page you can see download logs setting. These log files can be downloaded from Virtual machine using FTP.

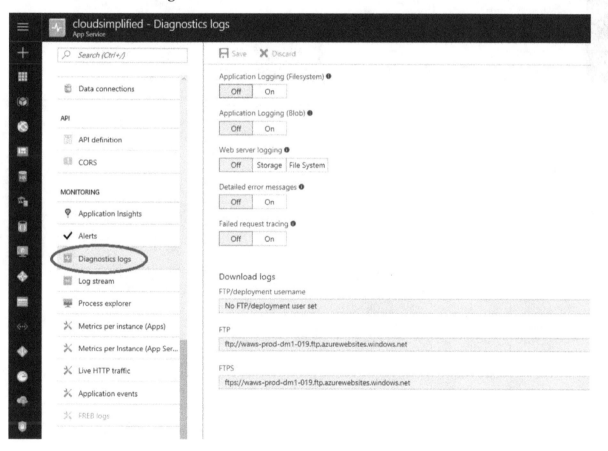

To get or set username/password for FTP, click "Deployment Credentials" under Deployment. You can set ftp username and password here.

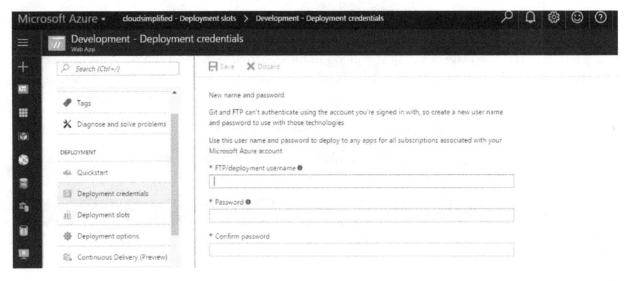

You can download logs using ftp or ARM. But what if you want to see live action. What if there is an issue with app and you want to see what is going on. In this scenario, you can use streaming logs. These are live logs. You can see these logs through Azure portal, Visual Studio or PowerShell.

You can go to Visual Studio server explorer. Connect to cloud and you should be able to see your apps in it. Select your web app, right click and you should be able to see "View Streaming Logs" option.

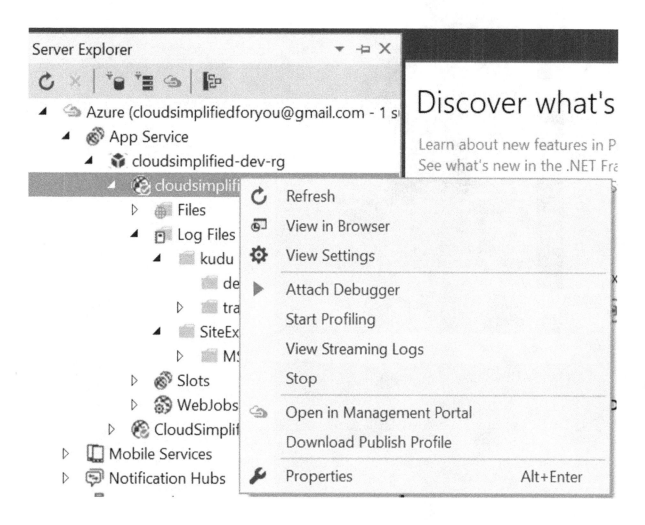

From the server explorer, you can download logs (as a zip), view streaming logs and some diagnostics settings.

Process Explorer

Under monitoring you can also see a link for process explorer. If you click on this link you can see w3wp process running on VM.

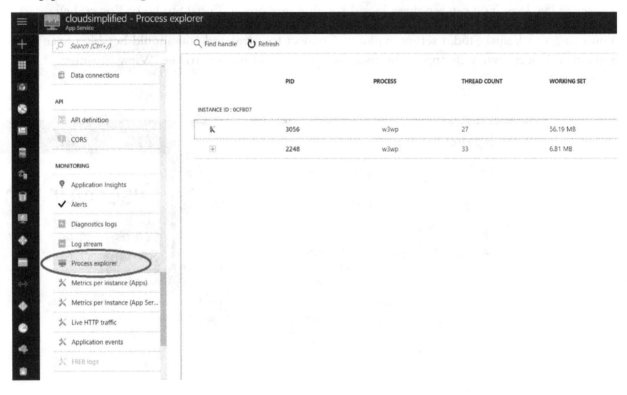

We have seen how we can download logs using FTP and Visual Studio Server Explorer. In this chapter, we will use kudu to download logs. Before using Kudu, I quickly wanted to show you "Console" option under development tools. When you click on it, a console window will open. It will connect "D:/home" folder on the underlying virtual machine.

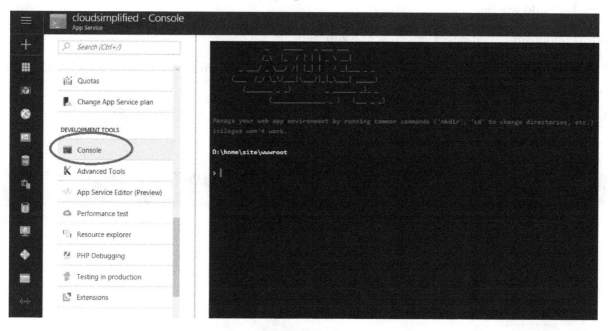

Kudu is a service that enables users to get list of running processes, their CPU and get logs. To connect to kudu just put "Scm" in front of your app. For example, if your website link is:

http://cloudsimplified-development.Azurewebsites.net/

Link for kudu will be

http://cloudsimplified-development.scm.Azurewebsites.net/

Lets put this link in web browser. As you can see there are lot of things we can do using Kudu. Click on the "Site Extensions" link.

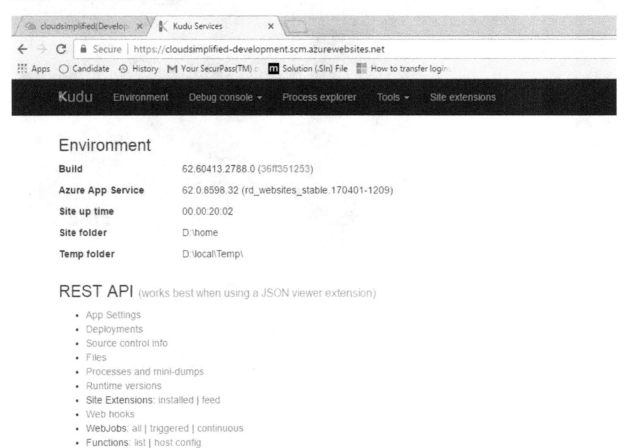

When you click "Site extensions" you will be presented with the following page. For our exercise, we will install "Azure Web Site Logs Browser" extension. Click on the "+" button as shown in snapshot below to install it.

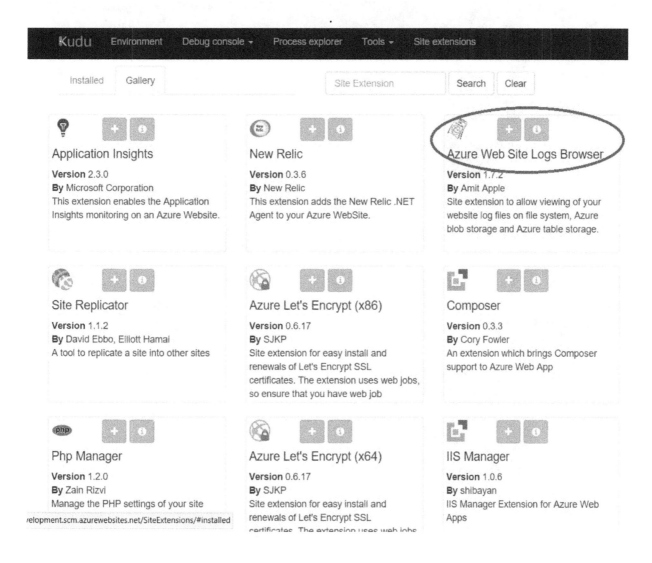

After you have installed the extension, click on the launch button to launch it.

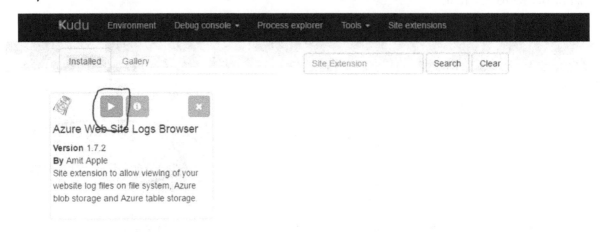

As seen below you can see "D:\Home\LogFiles" folder. Based on what logging you have enabled you will see folders under it.

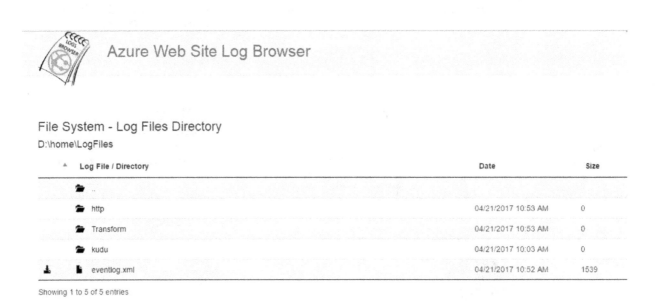

What gets swapped and what not

Now that we have learned about settings, logs, swapping of slots and certificates in web apps. It is time to find out what gets swapped and what stays with the slot when we do a slot swap.

Settings that SWAP	Setting that don't swap
General App Settings (like .NET framework)	End Points
Handler mappings	SSL Certificates
App Settings (Can be configured to stick to a slot)	Scaling Settings
Configuration Settings (Can be configured to stick to a slot)	Custom DNS Domain
Monitoring and Diagnostics settings	Web Job Scheduler
Web Jobs Content	

PowerShell provides commands that can be used for managing or interacting with resources in ARM. If you want to install PowerShell, you can do it from PowerShell Gallery. In this chapter, we will just look at few PowerShell commands. I highly recommend familiarizing yourself with basic PowerShell commands.

PowerShell Examples

Scenario 1: Deploy website using PowerShell. You can use this command if you have already created a package and want to deploy your app.

Command:

Publish-AzureWebsiteProject -Name site1 -Package .\webApplication.zip -slot 'development'

Scenario 2: Create a Service Plan using PowerShell

Command:

New-AzureRmAppServicePlan -ResourceGroupName 'cloudsimplified-dev-rg' -Name 'cloudsimplifiedappserviceplan' -Location "South Central US" -Tier Standard

Scenario 3: Create a Web App using PowerShell

Command:

New-AzureRmWebApp -ResourceGroupName Default-Web-WestUS -Name "cloudsimplified" -Location "South Central US" -AppServicePlan "cloudsimplifiedServicePlan"

Scenario 4: Create a Slot using PowerShell:

Command:

New-AzureRmWebApp -ResourceGroupName Default-Web-WestUS -Name " cloudsimplified " -Location "West US" -AppServicePlan "cloudsimplifiedServicePlan" -Slot "Development"

Scenario 5: Swap Slots

Command:

$paramterObject =@{targetSlot = "[slot name – 'dev']"}

Invoke-AzureRmResourceAction -ResourceGroupName [resource group name] -ResourceType Microsoft.Web/sites/slots -ResourceName [web app name]/ [Slot name] -Action slotsswap -Parameters $paramterObject

Scenario 6: Setting App Settings using PowerShell

Command:

$setting = @{'key' = 'value'; 'key2' ='value2'}

Set-AzureWebsite -Name '' -AppSettings $setting – ConnectionStrings $conn

Scenario 7: Delete a Slot

Command:

Remove-AzureRmResource -ResourceGroupName [resource group name] -ResourceType Microsoft.Web/sites/slots –Name [cloudsimplified]/[development]

THANK YOU

That's all I wanted to cover in this book. Thank you for reading my book. If you have any questions or suggestions related to book, feel free to email me at cloudsimplifiedforyou@gmail.com. Also, if you would like to get a notification when my next book on Virtual Machines is published, email at cloudsimplifiedforyou@gmail.com to be subscribed for the updates.